BUDDHISM FOR BEGINNERS

EVERYTHING YOU NEED TO KNOW ABOUT

BUDDHISM FOR COMPLETE BEGINNERS

ANZAN TASHI

Bonus: Download my Free E-book

I have written an E-Book that I believe will help anyone who wants to make a lasting change in their life. The title is 21 Day Total Life Transformation. All you have to do is go to JasonBracht.com enter your email address and I will deliver it directly to your inbox.

This resource will help you get the most out of life – I lay out step by step techniques that can help dig you out of any rut.

To get instant access to these incredible tools and resources, click the link below:

CLICK HERE FOR THE FREE 21 DAY TOTAL LIFE TRANSFORMATION BOOK

TABLE OF CONTENTS

WHAT IS BUDDHISM?

Buddhism can be called as a major global religion with a set of beliefs and a complex history. You can also look at it as a method of finding peace within your own self. It is a religion that enables you to discover your true happiness and contentment.

Buddhists develop kindness, inner peace and wisdom through daily practice; and then aim at sharing their experiences with others in order to bring real benefits to this world. The essence of Buddhism lies in making efforts not to harm others and to live gently and peacefully, working towards the ultimate goal of pure and lasting happiness for all living beings.

It can be expressed through the popular verse:

"Abandon negative action,

Create perfect virtue,

Subdue your own mind."

To put this in even simpler terms, you stop harming yourselves and others by abandoning negative actions such as killing, anger etc. and developing positive attitudes such as love and compassion, therefore creating a perfect virtue. You also work on subduing your mind through elimination of all false projections and understanding reality which makes you peaceful and calm.

Buddhism was founded by Buddha Shakyamuni who lived and taught in India some two and a half thousand years ago. A number of people around the world have discovered true happiness by following the pure spiritual path revealed by Buddha. The Buddhist way of life of kindness, peace and wisdom is just as relevant today as it was in the ancient India.

Some people refer to Buddhism as more of a philosophy or a *'way of life'* and not a religion. It is termed as philosophy because it means *'love of wisdom'* and can be summarized as:

- Leading a moral life
- Being mindful and aware of your thoughts and actions
- Developing understanding and wisdom

It explains your purpose to life, the apparent inequality and injustice in the world, and also provides a way of life that leads to true happiness and contentment.

WHO WAS THE BUDDHA?

The word 'Buddha' is derived from the ancient term 'Bodh' which means 'awakened.' Therefore, being Buddha would mean being awakened! And hence, _we can all be Buddha_.

Buddhism has witnessed many Buddha's or fully enlightened human beings. However, in Theravada Buddhism that is practiced in Southeast Asia, Buddha usually refers to the historical Buddha or Siddhartha Gotama who lived in India around 2500 years ago. Mahayana Buddhism is practiced in Tibet, China, Japan and Korea. This hints at a number of mythical Buddha's as well, each one of which is worshipped for the specific characteristics it symbolizes.

In this book, as we refer to Buddha, we shall talk about Siddhartha Gotama.

So, was Buddha a God?

Absolutely not! He was just a person whose consistent efforts led him to witness enlightenment. He was born to a royal family in Lumbini (now in Nepal) on a full moon day. He was lovingly called as Prince Siddhartha, and married a lovely princess called Yasodhara at the age of sixteen. Blessed with endless pleasure and privileges, Prince Siddhartha hadn't a care in the world.

His father was however extremely worried about his future. The reason for this was the manner in which various astrologers had predicted Prince Siddhartha's future. Shortly after he was born, the astrologers had told his father that Prince Siddhartha was either destined to be a great ruler or a Buddha. Now Siddhartha's father did not want his son to convert into a religious ascetic. Therefore, he shielded his son from every form of pain and ugliness, hoping to keep him ignorant of the world's suffering. He also tried to strengthen his son's attachment towards worldly pleasures.

This strategy worked for a few years. Then, one day Siddhartha went for a chariot ride through his kingdom. As he travelled through various places, he happened to witness an old man, a sick man, and a human corpse. He also saw a holy man. And there came the turning point in this life!

The very revelation that existence was contaminated by suffering impacted him so deeply that he became determined to leave his comfortable life in search for a lasting solution.

His wife had just given birth to their son and life seemed perfect by conventional standards. However, there were several questions in Siddhartha's mind. He asked himself, _"Why, being myself subject to birth, aging, ailment, death, sorrow and defilement, do I seek after what is also subject to these things? Suppose, being myself subject to these things, seeing the danger in them, I sought after the unborn, unaging, unailing, deathless, sorrowless, undefiled, supreme surcease of bondage, nibbana?" (Majjhima-nikaya 26.)_

For the next six year, Buddha wandered through India as a homeless wanderer and studied with the greatest spiritual masters of his age. At that time, it was believed that the highest spiritual state which Buddha was aiming for could be achieved only through the practice of self-mortification. Since Siddhartha was an extremely determined student, he was ready to follow any method in order to seek knowledge and enlightenment. He also practiced extreme fasting along with other austerities. Although he was on the brink of death, yet he was unafraid, because he believed that the time of death will make him reach the pinnacle he sought. However, after six years of striving hard, he did not reach close to his goal of total liberation from sufferings. His teachers considered him as their equal and his body was emaciated from the effort, yet he was determined to search for the truth. He resolved to begin his quest for truth and wisdom all by himself. He thought that if self-mortification was truly the path to enlightenment, he should have had reached it already. And this thought worried him!

Siddhartha remembered how once, when he was a child, he had entered into spontaneous meditation while sitting in the shade of a rose-apple tree. As he recollected that experience, he wondered if that could be the path to enlightenment. And it appeared as if it could be! He had gone as far as he could with both pain and pleasure. So, it occurred to him that only the Middle Way between the two extremes of self mortification or sensual pleasure could lead to freedom, Nirvana or Nibbana.

He realized that a weak body could not facilitate freedom of mind and hence, decided to abandon the practice of fasting. However, his eating little rice and bread instigated the five ascetics who had been his companions earlier to dessert him. These ascetics thought that Siddhartha could not continue his search and had therefore "reverted to luxury."

Meanwhile, Siddhartha regained his strength and a few days later sat down to meditate under the Bodhi tree with a strong determination that he would not rise until he reached a state of enlightenment. And finally, after meditating through the night, he witnessed the true nature of reality. He saw the workings of his own mind and eradicated all traces of hatred, greed and delusion. He then touched Nibbana or the deathless element that was immune to change or pain.

He was no longer Prince Siddhartha, but became Buddha Gotama, the Fully Awakened One. He understood that there had been many Buddha's before him and there would be many more in the future. He also knew that any human being who made the requisite effort to achieve enlightenment was capable of becoming a Buddha too.

Therefore, the word 'Buddha' refers to these human beings who have made substantial efforts and practice the principles of Buddhism.

The Buddha called his realizations of ultimate reality as "The Four Noble Truths." However, these truths were subtle and profound. They could only be experienced after diligent efforts. Therefore, he doubted if others in the society could understand these.

Now, as Buddha was thinking this, a heavenly being persuaded him to share his knowledge. Then something miraculous happened – Buddha saw the image of a lotus pool in his mind's eye. He inferred that, similar to the lotus flower where certain petals were sunk underwater and others rose above the surface, the minds of human beings performed at different levels. Some were stuck like the lotus petals under water while the others were ready to open in the light of dharma (or the truth). These individuals who were ready to open in the light of truth or law would be able to understand his teachings.

He explained his discovery to his former companions at the deer park in Isipatana (now called Sarnath). These five ascetics who had initially deserted him were skeptical in the beginning but during the course of time, decided to listen and eventually achieved enlightenment.

The next four and-a-half decades of Buddha's life were spent in spreading his teachings throughout India where he endeavored to explain the Middle Path and the Four Noble Truths to people who were ready to understand them, regardless of age, sex, wealth or caste. He opened his "dharma" to everyone including penniless lepers as well as the kings. In those times, nobody had heard about such an attitude of equality. The Buddha taught laymen, laywomen, monks, murderers and spirits about the sufferings in life and described the way to end this physical and mental distress. However, he could not deliberate enlightenment; he could only show the way! Each being was expected to figure out and walk the path for themselves.

The word 'Dhamma' or 'Dharma' refers to the teachings of Buddha. It is also mentioned in terms of 'the truth about all existence' as this is what Buddha wanted to teach.

The Buddha was not a personified God, nor was he the mouthpiece of a God. He did not claim to be divine or immortal. The profound knowledge that he possessed came from his personal realization of the truth and was not inspired by the Divine. That liberating truth could only be found within one's own self. Buddha discovered it within himself!

Buddha believed that anyone could gain liberation from suffering – all it required was simple effort and persistent hard work. The reward of this hard work was nibbana or nirvana and this seemed to be priceless. The path to enlightenment lay in practicing what he referred to as the Eight-fold path and the Middle Way. The practice of insight meditation or vipassana was the kingpin of that path. By following the technique of vipassana, one could develop the knowledge to pierce through illusions and perceive all phenomenon as they really were.

The Buddha never demanded blind loyalty from his disciples and advocated freedom of thought. He advised them to test his teachings for themselves and preached compassion and nonviolence. He was against killing or harming any creature, even an insect!

Buddha's psychic eye looked for people who he could help. During the course of time, the Buddha visited his father's palace with an intention to preach the dharma for the benefit of his family. Many of his family members, including his father, stepmother, former wife and son, achieved enlightenment under his guidance. One day, he ate a tainted dish called "hog's mincemeat" and fell gravely ill. He demonstrated remarkable compassion, even as he was dying.

Buddha passed away in the village of Kusinara at the age of eighty. His life is a testament to the power of the human mind.

His encouraging last words were an appeal to his disciples: "All conditioned things are impermanent - strive on with diligence!"

Keeping the legacy alive, today, more than five-hundred million people continue to strive!

Today, you may even look at Buddha as your omniscient mind expressing itself in certain physical aspects in order to communicate with you.

Yet another way is to view Buddha as the appearance of the future Buddha you want to become once you properly and completely engross yourself in the path to cleanse your mind and develop your potential.

BUDDHIST TRADITIONS

With its spread through Asia, the teachings of Buddhism came to be interpreted in many different ways. Different 'schools of thought' evolved with each one demonstrating its own distinct practice.

Although each school reflects some unique practices and belief systems, all share certain common and fundamental teachings of the Buddha.

Commonly, the Buddhist traditions are presented as three main "schools" — the Theravada, the Mahayana and the Vajrayana (or Tibetan Buddhism). Now, all these categories do have a useful purpose, but they also oversimplify the various differences within traditions along with highlighting the connection between various traditions. Let us look at these traditions in a little more detail:

THE THERAVADA SCHOOL OF THOUGHT

Theravadan (also referred to as the "Doctrine of the Elders") Buddhism traces its roots to the earliest traditions of Buddhism. It begins with the original Sangha of the Buddha and is considered as the only surviving representative of the earliest schools of Buddhism.

Theravadan Buddhists recognize the earliest collected teachings of the Buddha (called the Pali Canon), as the true and influential Dharma. (Pali was a language used during the Buddha's lifetime.) Almost all the branches of Buddhism recognize the suttas (teachings) of the Pali Canon and accept them as authentic; however some more teachings are also regarded as authentic in certain traditions.

Theravada Buddhism (sometimes called the Southern Buddhism) has over 100 million followers. The religion was taken to a number of countries, primarily by the Buddhist missionaries from India. However, in the initial stages, it achieved a foothold in Sri Lanka only. During the course of years, it spread from Sri Lanka to Burma, Thailand, Cambodia, Laos, and certain parts of Vietnam.

The Theravadans believe that the ideal Buddhist is the "one who is worthy". They profoundly worship or regard the historical Buddha as a perfected master. However, they do not pay homage to the various Buddha's and Bodhisattvas that are worshiped in the Mahayana.

A new form of Theravadan practice centered on meditation has taken root in the West. This is termed as Vipassana or insight meditation. It was brought to the west by Westerners who trained in India, Burma and with teachers such as Ajahn Chah and Mahasi Saydaw.

The insight meditation does not propagate a belief system. It only highlights a technique that can enable one to see clearly through the nature of his mind. It refers to practices of the mind that can develop insight through reflection and calm through sustained attention.

THE MAHAYANA SCHOOL OF THOUGHT

Mahayana Buddhism has been historically practiced in the Far East and in North Asia, including Japan, China, Tibet, Korea and Mongolia. A number of Mahayana traditions are now being established in the West as well.

Mahayana refers to a movement that was initiated in the first century C.E. It described itself as the "great vehicle". There is still some controversy around the differences between both the movements. Here are some agreed upon distinctions:

- Both the Theravadans and the Mahayana Buddhists view the Pali Canon as a sacred scripture.
- The ultimate purpose of life for the Theravadan Buddhists is to strive to become an arhant – defined as an aspiration suitable only to monks and nuns. However, the Mahayana Buddhists wish to become boddhisatvas who can be regarded as saints who have achieved enlightenment and yet delay nirvana unselfishly in order to help others attain it as well. This is similar to what Buddha practiced.
- The paths for attaining enlightenment also differ in the two schools of thoughts. The Mahayana Buddhists believe that enlightenment can be achieved even by a layperson and is possible to be attained in a single lifetime.
    The practice is of Bodhicitta, or the Bodhi Heart is considered as supreme in the Mahayana school of thought.
- Some Mahayana traditions are more religious in nature than the Theravadan rituals. Again, this cannot be generalized as both have their specific traditions.
- Another worth noting thing is that although both the Mahayana and Thervadan schools of thought assert that theirs is the more authentic form of Buddhism, they work together peacefully in some great learning monasteries such as Nalanda.

There are several sects and schools within the Mahayana tradition:

Zen: Zen lays stress on the prime importance of the experience of enlightenment, which is incommunicable and indefinable, free from all concepts and forms. Only an enlightened individual can test the authenticity of the enlightenment experience.

Zen also encourages the practice of zazen, or sitting in meditative absorption. This is considered as the shortest but also the steepest way to awakening.

Pure Land Traditions: The Pure Land tradition stresses on the recitation of the name of Amitabha (or the Buddha of Infinite Light). This is considered as a mechanism that leads to his Pure Land of Happiness, a kind of paradise in which everything is favorable for becoming a Buddha.

Nichiren Buddhism: This is also referred to as the New Lotus School and is based on the Lotus Sutra. The founder of this practice, Nichiren, mentions that the title of the Lotus Sutra alone contains the essence of all Buddhist teachings.

This practice encourages recitation of the formula, *"Veneration to the Sutra of the Lotus of the Good Law" (Nam-myoho-renge-kyo)*. A dedicated recitation of this formula can lead to instant realization.

THE VAJRAYANA SCHOOL OF THOUGHT

The Vajrayana Buddhism and Tibetan Buddhism are often confused. Tibetan Buddhism can be referred to a kind of Mahayana Buddhism with its roots in Tibet and the Himalayan region. It combines the Mahayana philosophy, Tantric symbolic rituals, meditation and the Theravadan monastic discipline. It can be called as a form of Mahayana Buddhism and incorporates the practice of tantra (or Vajrayna).

The Vajrayana or "Diamond Vehicle" (also called as Tantrayana, Tantric, Mantrayana, or esoteric Buddhism) incorporates many of the basic concepts of Mahayana. Along with this, it also includes a vast collection of spiritual techniques designed to magnify the Buddhist practice. A main component of the Vajrayana school of thought is to harness a person's psycho-physical energy as a means to develop a profound state of awareness and concentration. This state can then be used as an efficient path to Buddhahood. The Vajrayana Buddhists also recognize a large body of texts that include the Buddhist Tantras.

Similar to all other religions, Buddhism aims to provide us with hope. However, unlike other religions, it teaches us to search for hope within ourselves instead of looking for it from outside. Considering this factor, Buddhism may not be considered as a religion. **It is simply a belief in your own self – a belief that you can tread the path to self fulfilment and ultimate enlightenment.**

THE THREE TREASURES OR JEWELS OF BUDDHISM

The Three Jewels or the three treasures of Buddhism lay the foundation of Buddhism.

The first jewel is the **_Buddha_**. The word 'Buddha' implies 'the Awakened One.' It does not necessarily mean the Prince Siddhartha or Shakyamuni Buddha who achieved enlightenment in the sixth century before the Common Era in India or 'historical Buddha.' In fact, all those who have blossomed into their full potential post awakening from the sleep of ignorance are referred to as the 'Buddha.'

Blossomed and awakened, they become teachers for others and are therefore instrumental in awakening others as well. This is considered as an extremely role. It should be understood that freedom from suffering, liberation, awakening, awareness and Buddhahood – are all a result of your own understanding. All these actually provide an insight into your own reality. No magical empowerment can help you discover these. Nor can these be discovered through some sort of a secret gimmick or group membership. It is not even possible to achieve enlightenment solely by faith, although some good faith always helps. Meditation can help but just meditation may not lead to an awakened state.

Therefore, the most significant element of Buddha is that Buddha is a teacher, and he is instrumental in leading us towards a path of enlightenment. This teaching cannot be called as indoctrination; it does not impose any beliefs. Rather, it provides us with a methodology that can be deployed to develop ourselves, to meditate upon, to learn and think over, and finally, to gain profound, deep, transforming wisdom, insight or understanding.

Hence, it is natural to _take refuge in the Buddha_: _Namo buddham sharanam gacchami._ It becomes natural to turn towards the teachings that lead to the reality of pleasure. This is actually teaching of the method that enables us to achieve happiness and pleasure in whatever form it comes to us – this may be in the form of Christianity, humanism, Sufism, Hinduism or Buddhism. Here, the form doesn't matter because, the teacher is the 'Buddha' – he is the one who can direct us to our own reality. Here 'Buddha' could be a religious teacher or a scientist. It does not matter!

The second jewel of Buddhism is the **Dharma**. We tend to take refuge in the Dharma: Namo dharmam sharanan gacchami.

The meaning of the word 'Dharma' is 'to be held.' It points towards the reality itself! Although it has a number of other meanings beyond this reality too!

The greatest meaning of Dharma is the reality that holds us in initiating freedom from suffering – this reality holds us in a state of delight, pleasure, happiness or pure bliss! We can call Dharma as our own reality that we endeavor to fully understand. It can therefore be said that the mechamism and the teachings of this mechanism that enables us to open ourselves constitutes the 'Dharma.' It includes all the practices that we follow, all the practices that can deepen our understanding of self, the teachings that allow us to open ourselves and implementation of those practices and teachings in our lives.

We can say that our ethics and virtues also constitute the Dharma. The qualities that we develop and those that lead us towards our quest for freedom and reality also constitute Dharma. This is why Dharma is implied as religion in some contexts. It means "duty" and other kinds of procedures and habits in Vedic Brahmanism. Buddha was the first one to use this word in a liberating manner.

Human beings ultimately take refuge in reality itself. This is because reality is the only perfectly safe refuge. All unrealistic things are capable of destruction; they can be blown away by the howling wind. However, reality cannot be blown away. It is real! It is there to stay! It is uncreated! It lasts! It is present and therefore capable of providing refuge!

The final taking of refuge happens when we personify reality in our existence – we realize that this reality is our thought, mind, breath and body! Therefore, the final refuge happens through being Buddha ourselves. However, during this process, we do take refuge in reality – the second jewel of Buddhism.

The third jewel of Buddhism is the _**'Sangha,'**_ or the community of individuals who enjoy these treasures of refuge and who believe in the teachings of the Buddha. They seek the understanding of the principles that can be deployed in the practice of Dharma. These individuals consciously evolve towards being 'Buddha's,' and share their knowledge, understanding and bliss with each other. They are committed to help people discover these jewels.

All Buddhists chant the below mantra, each in their own language:

Namo buddham sharanam gacchami. Namo dharmam sharanam gacchami. Namo sangham sharanam gacchami.

The word 'Namo' implies 'I bow' – this would in reality imply that 'I bow to express faith, trust and respect' The word 'Buddham' would mean 'to the Buddha' 'Sharanam' would imply 'refuge' and 'gacchami' would mean 'I go'. 'Namo buddham sharanam gacchami' would therefore mean 'I bow to Buddha and resort to him as refuge.' This resort is like going for some relaxation in order to restore your energy and attain some peace. The word 'sharanam' would mean 'a person who goes to refuge' from sufferings. Some people refer to this as 'ascetic' but we can also understand this one as a 'vacationer' or somebody who goes for a break. 'Dharmam sharanam gacchami,' would imply that 'I take refuge in reality.' 'Sangham sharanam gacchami,' would mean that 'I take refuge in the community.' Or that I would join likeminded people who are also taking a break like me.

The Buddha's teachings can be viewed as a building with its own distinct stories, foundation and roofs. Similar to all other buildings, this building (or the teachings of Buddha) also has a door and this door is through the refuge in three jewels – in the Buddha or the enlightened teacher, in Dharma or the truth and in the Sangha or the community!

By taking refuge in Buddha, you learn the art of transforming anger into compassion.

By taking refuge in Dharma, you master the art of transforming delusion into wisdom.

By taking refuge in Sangha, you can transform desire into generosity.

It must be remembered that taking refuge will not bring any supernatural powers to you. The power to achieve ultimate enlightenment or awakening is a result of your own efforts, sincerity and commitment.

THE THREE POISONS OR ROOTS OF EVIL IN BUDDHISM

Buddhism mentions that the cause of all human suffering is ***anger, greed and ignorance.*** These fundamental evils or negative traits are referred to as the three poisons or the 'roots of evil' in Buddhism. These are considered to be toxic and dangerous for human life. Not only do these three poisons form a source of the human mind's unquenchable thirst for worldly pleasures or become the root cause of all societal evil, but they are also painful pollutants that can cause physical and mental ill-health!

Lust and desire are considered to be the companions of greed and they lead us to 'get hold of' things and possess more and more of them!

Hatred and aversion can be considered as anger's best friends and these lead us to reject anything that displeases us.

Ignorance strengthens our belief in something that is non real or false.

These three evils can fill your life with unhappiness, suffering and dissatisfaction. They will lead you to make non skillful decisions that can impact your future. They may even encourage dishonest intentions that can lead you to act unethically. Over time, these three evils not only remain a cause of your own pain and agony but also impact your loved ones and the society.

Buddhism does provide a solution to end these three evils. Kindness and compassion can help you eradicate these contaminants and enlightenment can serve as the perfect antidote.

Most of us are dominated by one of these poisons. And when one poison becomes the dominating poison, the other two silently wait to be nourished.

Dominance of anger may lead to depression or obsession over real or imaginary enemies, political views and other negative realities of life.

Dominance of greed can be demonstrated by self-indulgence and lack of compassion.

Dominance of ignorance leads to insecurity, powerlessness and apathy.

The Buddhist teachings believe that the three evils are demonstrated in the society as a result of our interconnectedness. Greed can lead to destruction in the environment and anger can lead to injustice.

Awareness of the three poisons and strategies to cure them can bring about an amazing metamorphosis. The practice of compassion and kindness can convert these bitter poisons into sweet nectars, resulting in true happiness!

THE FIVE PERCEPTS OF BUDDHISM

Similar to the three jewels that form a simple framework for transmission of the Buddhist philosophy, the five percepts serve as ethical guidelines for the followers of this philosophy.

It must be understood that these five percepts are not a rigid set of rules. They are not the ten Buddhist commandments. Rather, they provide a practical basis to a good and ethical lifestyle that produces the right environment which enables you to seek out your own truth.

THE FIRST PERCEPT OR NOT KILLING:

The first percept is about not killing living beings intentionally. Now, we do sometimes step on ants and occasionally beat the odd cockroach to oblivion. Avoiding this may not be possible. However, according to the first percept, pre-medicated killing of fellow humans and senseless killing of animals for the purpose of sports and pleasure is absolutely non desirable. This percept aims at developing a concern for welfare and safety of others through compassion and selflessness.

The Theravada School of thought mentions that violation of the first precepts must involve five factors.

1. There is a living being
2. There is a perception that the being is a living being
3. There is a violent thought of killing
4. The killing is carried out
5. The being dies

When you observe the first percept, you try to protect life – as much as possible!

Now, this may lead you to believe that Buddhism discourages _services in the armed forces_ since this may amount to killing. Well, you would be surprised to know that approximately 3,000 Buddhists serve in the U.S armed forces today. This is because Buddhism does not demand absolute pacifism. However, it does encourage one to be skeptical if war is 'just' and necessary. Buddhism does mention that the collective ego of the nation may be subject to the poisons of hatred, greed and ignorance and therefore encourage war. It discourages an individual to get involved in this kind of a war and therefore encourages him to make informed decisions.

People often associate Buddhism with _vegetarianism_. Almost all Buddhist schools of thought encourage vegetarianism, it is considered to be a personal choice. In fact, the historical Buddha himself was not a strict vegetarian and asked his monks to eat anything, including meat. However, the monks were encouraged to refuse meat if they knew that the animal had been slaughtered just to feed the monks. The leftover meat of an animal that was slaughtered to feed a lay family was accepted by the monks. Certain kinds of meat such as meat of horse, dog, elephant, tiger, snake, bear and leopard were forbidden to be consumed.

Today, the Mahayana Buddhists propagate strict vegetarianism whereas the Theravada Buddhists leave it as more of a personal choice.

Since the Buddha believed in the middle way, Buddhists who practice vegetarianism are advised not to get fanatically attached to the belief.

Let me try and explain this with an example here: Let us say that you are visiting your grandmother's place after a gap of few years. Since it has been a long time, your grandmother decides to prepare your once-upon-a-time favorite dish: stuffed chicken breasts! You loved these when you were a child and this is all she remembered while she cooked these. Her frail body cannot get into the kitchen to cook something else and she has poured all her love into the dish that she has prepared. If you hesitate to consume this dish even once, then you are not a true Buddhist!

Buddhism considers _abortion_ as killing. However, Buddhists are generally hesitant to intervene in woman's personal decision to terminate her pregnancy. Although they discourage abortion, yet they encourage the middle path and are therefore not too rigid with beliefs and traditions.

If we look at the world around us today, we can easily say that we are killing every day. Vegetables and fruits are derived from living organisms and farming requires killing rodents and insects that may destroy the plants. The heating in our houses may be causing harm to the environment and the cars that we drive are not eco-friendly too! As a Buddhist, your role is to not mindlessly follow the rules mentioned in the book, but to be mindful of the harm that you are causing to life and environment and do your best to minimize it.

THE SECOND PERCEPT OF NOT STEALING:

The second percept of Buddhism is translated as 'do not steal' or 'practice generosity'. It is more to do with taking only what has been given to you and implies that you return all the borrowed items. You are discouraged to take unfair advantage of situations or individuals and instill within yourself a sense of fair play and generosity towards the society.

Now, most individuals view stealing as 'theft'. However there are situations where you are not committing a theft and yet taking unfair advantage of people or circumstances around you. An example of this could be a software firm owner who uses the services of a particular contractor for three months and then fires him, only to hire another one. She does the same thing with the other contractor whom she has hired and then hires yet another one. Now, this is ethically permitted by law – she can change her service provider or the contractor whenever she wants to. But here is what she is actually doing – she is using the services of the contractor for the first three months which is the free service period and then fires the contractor, only to use the services of some other contractor for the next three months. This other contractor also meets with the same fate post three months. Although she is allowed by law to replace her contractor after the 'cool off' or 'free service period', in this situation she is using the law to take unfair advantage of the system as well as people. Had the contractors known that they would not get a permanent contract with her firm, they would have never agreed for the first three months services as well. This is 'stealing' according to the second percept of Buddhism. If we pay attention to this percept, we also get the realization that by not stealing we actually imply 'not taking advantage of another person's property or situation, not exploiting individuals and practicing generosity.'

THE THIRD PERCEPT OR NOT MISUSING SEX:

Almost every religion lays down some concrete rules for sexual conduct. The third percept in Buddhism can be interpreted as 'Do not misuse sex' or 'Do not indulge in sexual misconduct'. However, the ancient scriptures did not mention what constitutes sexual misconduct.

Now, most monks and nuns do not engage in sexual intercourse and are automatically expelled from the 'order' if this percept is not adhered to. A monk is not allowed to make any suggestive comments towards a woman and nuns must not allow any man to fondle, touch or rub them anywhere between the knees and the collar bone.

During the ancient times, this rule was followed in almost all countries during the ancient times (with exception of Japan). Japanese Buddhist monks did marry and this was not considered to be an infrequent exception.

If we analyze this percept today, we can safely say that any kind of non-consensual or exploitative sex would constitute sexual misconduct. According to Buddhism, sex between two individuals who love each other is considered as 'moral' or 'ethical'. This is irrespective of the fact whether these individuals are married or not.

Tibetan Buddhism discourages gay marriages. Anti-homosexual teachings are incorporated by some other schools of Buddhism too. However, the historical Buddha never addressed the question of homosexuality specifically.

You will read in the Second noble truth that the cause of all sufferings is desire. Now, this does not imply that all desire is bad and should be suppressed. In fact, the Buddhist practice encourages you to acknowledge your passions and win over them. They should not be in a position to control you and you must be able to utilize the energy of this desire as a source for enlightenment.

Various schools of Buddhism go to extremes when they talk about abstinence from sex. There are others that term this energy as a fuel for awakening or enlightenment. As a true Buddhist, you could follow the middle path because the historical Buddha was never too rigid about rules and encouraged the use of middle path!

THE FOURTH PERCEPT OR NOT LYING:

The fourth Buddhist percept encourages one to not speak falsely, gossip aimlessly, lie or misrepresent people or situations in a discussion. It emphasizes on the use of kind and truthful conversation filled with positive intentions. This percept has also been called as 'practice truthfulness' or 'abstain from falsehood.'

The Theravada school of Buddhism identifies four elements that can violate the fourth percept.

1. Any situation that seems to be untrue or worth lying about
2. Any intention that leads to deceiving
3. Any gestures or body language that display and expression of falsehood
4. Any other kind of false impression

Any kind of speech rooted in the three poisons – hatred, greed and ignorance, is considered as false speech. If you speak because you want to get something, hurt someone or make you seem more important than anybody else, it would be classified as false speech.

Truth comes from compassion and mindfulness. In order to tell the truth, you need to be aware of what is the truth. Sometimes, not speaking up is also considered as false speech. I would like to take an example of a renowned educator here. For the past five years, this educator had been sexually exploiting small children. However, his staff who knew about it chose to maintain silence in order to protect their jobs. This choice of maintaining silence in a wrongful deed must be regarded as false speech.

Deploying the fourth percept in your life is a deep practice that can influence your mind and body. It can also serve as a great gift to others.

THE FIFTH PERCEPT OR NOT ABUSING INTOXICANTS:

This seems to be the most important percept in today's affluent society. This percept talks about avoiding intoxicants such as alcohols, drugs and stimulants such as tea and coffee. This percept enables development of rational thinking and inner clarity required to bring in mindfulness. Almost all Buddhist schools of thoughts believe that consuming liquor is a violation of the fifth percept.

If we want to relate this percept to the modern day society, we can define intoxicants as something that manipulates your real self or experience. Therefore, this would not really imply abstinence from coffee, tea or chewing gum. However, if you are using these as intoxicants, then this is definitely a violation of the fifth percept.

THE TEN GRAND PERCEPTS

The Mahayana Buddhists follow a list of ten principles or percepts. These are found in the Brahma Net Sutra or the Mahayana Sutra. Here are the ten percepts:

1. Do not indulge in killing
2. Do not indulge in stealing
3. Do not misuse sex
4. Do not lie
5. Do not indulge in intoxicant abuse
6. Do not talk about others' errors and faults
7. Do not elevate yourself and blame others
8. Do not become stingy
9. Do not get angry
10. Do not speak ill of the three treasures

The Mahayana Buddhists also believe in the **Three Pure Percepts**. These are:

1. Do no evil
2. Do good
3. Save all beings

Do not get overwhelmed if you hear about the **Sixteen Bodhisattva Vows** or **Sixteen Bodhisattva Percepts**. These only refer to the ten grand percepts, the three pure percepts and the three refuges, namely:

'I shall take refuge in the Buddha

I shall take refuge in the Dharma

I shall take refuge in the Sangha'

THE FOUNDATION OF BUDDHISM – THE FOUR NOBLE TRUTHS

Buddha's first lecture after attaining enlightenment was centered around the Four Noble Truths, which are treated as the foundation of Buddhism. These truths enable the devotees to attain their own enlightenment or Nirvana which is the sole aim of Buddhism. Nirvana is a state in which one achieves mastery of mind, complete freedom and peace of mind. The state of Nirvana can be compared to a 'heaven on earth'. It is important to remove feelings of greed, anger, selfishness and any other negative emotions from your life if you want to achieve Nirvana.

It is believed that as Buddha rose from his meditative state, he was hesitant to share his wisdom with other individuals because he was unsure if everybody could grasp this wisdom. He started sharing his knowledge based on the advice from his fellowmen. His faith in his fellowmen has given us access to the Buddhist principles.

The four noble truths were the first principles that Buddha shared with the people who wanted to achieve Nirvana. The truths are:

1. The truth of suffering (dukkha)
2. The truth of the cause of suffering (samudaya)
3. The truth of the end of suffering (nirhodha)
4. The truth of the path that frees us from suffering (magga)

The *first noble truth* implies that living means 'dukkha'. 'Dukkha' is that feeling of deep discontentment or suffering – Why am I not happy today? I wanted to achieve this, why is it taking so long? Why can I not experience pleasure in everything that I do? All these questions translate into the first noble truth – Dukkha. There is no doubt that human life is filled with difficulties, pain and trouble. And acceptance of this truth can lead you to begin your journey to Nirvana. Even if you are blessed with a happy and contended life, you need to prepare yourself for this harsh truth. Simply believing in this truth can prepare you for the hard journey ahead.

The second noble truth details the cause of Dukkha. This is Desire. Wouldn't you be happier if things were a little different today, if you had a little more money and a little more time? This feeling of general dissatisfaction arising out of desire translates into the second noble truth. Desire comes in three forms: ignorance, greed and hatred. A man's ignorance can make him desire for success without being truly aware of what is going on inside his own mind. His obsession for material possessions, power and control can be instrumental in converting his desire into greed. His emotions such as anger and hatred may begin to control him in case he becomes really attached to them.

The third noble truth throws light on how you can eradicate suffering. It mentions that elimination of desire can lead to elimination of suffering. It is simple – remove the cause to stop the effect. Now, this does not imply that you give up your worldly pleasures, your relationships, hard work, job or life. It just implies that you give up that fruitless grasping and that painful longing. You need to give up the feeling of desire – because that feeling of not having something causes pain. Agreed - suffering exists in the real world! However, you do not need to suffer if you do not wish to! You do not need to pretend to be what you are not! All your focus should be on how you can get rid of the hatred, ignorance and greed in your life.

The fourth noble truth describes the eightfold path to give up desire by living the middle way. This is the way that Buddha suggested. This is the way that can bring more peace and happiness into your life. While the third truth mentions that it is possible to eradicate suffering, the fourth truth shows the path to do so. This path is really mindfulness meditation but can be further broken down into the eightfold path.

LIVING THE BUDDHIST PHILOSOPHY: THE EIGHTFOLD PATH

Through the four noble truths, Buddha described that elimination of desires can lead to an elimination of suffering. The Eightfold Path describes the rules you should follow in order to achieve this. These are some critical principles that all Buddhists are encouraged to learn and practice. Practicing this path can be your cure for suffering. These principles are often referred to as a path, but it is not necessary to follow them one after another. They should just be treated like your practical guide to live the Buddhist philosophy. They are a framework that can make life easier for you.

We can group these eight principles into three categories:

- **WISDOM**: The first two steps (Right View and Right Intention) can be grouped under this category.
- **MORAL CONDUCT**: The next three steps (Right Speech, Right Action and Right Livelihood) fall under this category.
- **FOCUS**: These are the final three steps of the Eight fold part and are the most difficult to attain. These include Right Effort, Right Mindfulness and Right Concentration.

Let us try and understand all the eight steps:

1. Right View

This implies that you should aim at understanding yourself and the world. You should be aware of the actions that you take and the reasons that lead to those actions. You must develop an understanding of the four noble truths and view the world as it really is. Understand that nothing is permanent – everything changes and clinging to something (desire) is an illusion that will only lead to unhappiness.

2. Right Intention

You must be sure about what is controlling your actions. Are you looking at everybody's benefit or just your own self? Do not act upon feelings of aggression, desire or prejudgment.

3. Right Speech

You should be careful about your choice of words. Understand that your choice of words can make or break lives. Therefore never speak deliberate lies. Do not speak harsh words that can hurt or offend others. Only use a positive and friendly tone while you speak.

4. Right Action

This one is really simple: You should not do any wrong. You should practice non-violence and not indulge in animal killing. Do not exploit others by stealing or sexually misusing them, do not exploit your senses by lustful eating or intoxication. Now, this does not imply that you abstain yourself from that lovely glass of wine that you prefer to have with your meal. It simply means having more control and knowing when to stop.

5. Right Livelihood

This means that you should aim at living a meaningful life and indulge in jobs that demand honesty, love and compassion. Do not do any job because it gets you some fast cash. Choose your occupation carefully.

The jobs that should be avoided are:
- weapon trade
- trade in living beings for slavery, prostitution or meat production
- drugs and alcohol trade
- any job that does not adhere to the principles of right action and right speech

6. Right Effort

Effort is the steering wheel for all the other aspects in the Eightfold philosophy of Zen. Nothing can be accomplished if you do not put in the right kind of effort. This means refraining from things that can cause harm, eliminating negative thoughts and tendencies along with indulging in actions that can lead to betterment of the society. Always aim at cultivating positive thoughts that can lead to positive actions and focus your efforts on where some good can be done.

7. Right Mindfulness

This focusses on being mindful or attentive. You need to be mindful of yourself, your feelings, body language, surroundings, ideas and thoughts and things that are happening around you. Think about the present, always be focused, alert and attentive. Do not try and judge things or people. Live in the present.

8. Right Concentration

This implies that you should focus on one thing at a time. Whatever you are doing, just ensure that you are concentrating on that wholeheartedly. Do not let your mind wander or get distracted. Right concentration can be achieved through Zazen (Meditation). However, meditation can help you achieve one-pointedness of mind during the process of meditation. It is for you to maintain this one pointedness in everything that you say or do.

Do remember that these are just guidelines. They are not carved out in stone and should not be followed like a numbered list. The good thing about Buddhism is the faith it has on the human mind. You know what is right and what is wrong. You just need to learn to view this with clarity. And Buddhists believe that clarity can be learnt through meditation (don't worry, this book contains a chapter on the right way to meditate too!).

The steps in the Eightfold path share some similarity with other Abrahamic religious beliefs that reiterate the importance of positive thinking and positive actions to sustain life. The main difference lies in the logic behind each principle.

The ultimate aim of Buddhism is Nirvana and this hugely differs from the concept of heaven explained in Christianity.

Through his teachings, the Buddha has described ways to eliminate sufferings. These are very different from the ways described in Christianity where it is believed that Jesus Christ or God can save man from his sins and take him to heaven. However, the _Buddha believed that man can overcome his sufferings while on earth and the power to do this rests with man himself._

A DAY IN THE LIFE OF A BUDDHIST

Before we look at a day in the life of a modern day Buddhist, let us look at how the Buddha spent his day. Well, Buddha divided his daily routine into five parts:

- The morning session
- The afternoon session
- The first watch
- The middle watch and
- The last watch

The Morning Session (between 4.00 a.m. to 12.00 noon)

Buddha's morning session involved the practice of meditation. The Buddha would wake up at 4.00 a.m. and sit down to meditate for an hour. The next one hour (from 5:00am to 6:00am) was focused on observing the world with his mental eye in order to understand if anybody needed help. He would put on his robe at around 6:00am and move out to either beg for food or help the needy.

Buddha normally went from house to house begging for food. His eyes would be fixed on the ground and he would receive any food that was put in his bowl in silence and with full gratitude. At times, he went with his disciples who walked with him in a single line. Sometimes, people would invite Buddha into their house for lunch and he would address them, in an effort to spread his wisdom and knowledge.

The Afternoon Session (between 12noon to 6.00 p.m.)

The afternoon session was focused around Buddha spreading his knowledge through his teachings. The monks would visit him to seek answers to various questions and he would happily oblige them. He would then retire into his room and view the world through his mental lens. This would be an attempt to find out who needed help. Post this; Buddha would meet various people who would be waiting to hear his teachings. He would teach them in a manner that everybody got equal attention. The wise experienced joy in his teachings, the average benefited their intelligence and the dull witted could rise from the dark – all through his teachings!

The   First   Watch (between   6.00   p.m.   to   10.00   p.m.)

This time was strictly reserved for Buddha's followers who would either seek solutions to their problems   or   hear   his   views   on   various   topics.   .

The   Middle   Watch (between   10.00   p.m.   to   2.00   a.m.)

This period was reserved for the Devas who would seize the opportunity to visit the Buddha and understand the truth of life.

The Last Watch (2.00 a.m. to 4.00 a.m.)

The first one hour of the last watch was spent in walking up and down in an effort to ease him from the ordeal of sitting the entire day. He would meditate by walking up and down and then sleep for an hour.

Now, this proves that Buddha was a busy man who only slept for one hour in a day. He believed in helping the world and during the early hours of the day looked at the universe, blessed it with his never ending love and brought happiness to a million hearts.

Alright, now do not begin to think that you would be required to practice a similar lifestyle. With the challenges of the modern day world, it is not possible to mimic Buddha's daily routine and follow it as it is.

HERE ARE SOME GUIDELINES TO A MODERN BUDDHIST LIFESTYLE:

DAILY LIFE AND SPIRITUALISM

Alright, so you are one of those who think that spiritual life is not so nice, it is mundane – it probably doesn't even exist, it is a mystical reality, it is something up there in the sky? Right? Quite often, people mention that they would need to neglect or ignore their everyday life and enter into a different kind of a spiritual world. Only then can they be really spiritual! Well, I feel that being a spiritual person simply implies being a real human being. And this is what Buddhism preaches too!

A well-known Vietnamese monk names Thich Nhat Hanh, has mentioned *"It is not so important whether you walk on water or walk in space. The true miracle is to walk on earth."* This is so true and beautifully relates to the present day lifestyle. It just means that the greatest miracle once can perform is to become a kind human being.

Therefore, it is absolutely fine if you have not experienced God talking to you directly. Because true miracles only happen when you become kind human beings. Even if you possessed certain psychic powers that enabled you to talk to God but lacked a kind heart, these powers would be of no use! Sometimes, they could even turn disadvantageous.

UPON WAKING UP

Is it possible to cultivate a kind heart? Yes, very much!

The question we need to ask ourselves is how?

Can you just cultivate a kind heart by getting up in the morning and reminding yourself of the things that you should or should not do? Absolutely not! The 'shoulds' normally remain as 'shoulds' and never get done. They also fill you up with guilt of not doing what you 'should' be doing! You can simply overcome the 'should' syndrome by understanding how you can transform your mind. When you understand the disadvantages of being self-centered, you develop a wish to become kind hearted. Thus automatically transforms your actions.

What do you think about the first thing as you get up in the morning? Is it about the food you would consume as breakfast or the manner in which you would handle that obnoxious jerk at work? Well, try and change this to something more positive. Something that helps set a positive tone for a kind day. How about reminding yourself that you will be kindhearted the entire day by not harming anyone, trying to be of service to others and by performing actions that can enable you to spread happiness amongst people around you?

This kind of a positive motivation is extremely beneficial, especially if set first thing in the morning. Did you know that your mind is really delicate and subtle when you wake up in the morning? Setting a positive motivation at this time elevates the chances of it staying with you and influencing you throughout the day.

Get out of bed after generating this positive tone for the day, wash yourself, have a cup of tea or coffee if you need and begin to recite prayers or meditate. This start to the day will bring you in touch with yourselves and empower you to become your own friend through continuous reinforcement of good qualities.

FINDING TIME TO MEDITATE EACH DAY

You do face challenges in finding time to meditate each day, don't you? Well, do you also face similar challenges in finding time to watch TV or go shopping? Probably not! If you can find time for all other activities, then twenty four hours should not seem like a short duration when it comes to finding time to meditate. You will only be able to find this time if you understand the value of spiritual practice. When you begin to realize the value that spiritual practice holds in your life, meditation and prayer becomes a high priority in your life and you definitely find time for it – just as you would find time for TV and shopping!

You could begin by setting up a daily meditation practice of 15 or 30 minutes early in the morning. This may even involve that 'incredible sacrifice' of giving up thirty minutes of TV so that you can get up a little early next morning. Treat meditation like food for your soul. Just as food nourishes the body, meditation nourishes you spiritually. And this nourishment leads you to begin respecting yourself as a human being.

MORNING MEDITATION

It is recommended that you begin your morning meditation session with a few prayers and an unselfish wish to help others. This can be followed by breathing meditation where you are required to sit calmly and experience your breath nourishing you. You must live in the present moment and let all negative thoughts and worries fade away. You may want to chant your favorite Buddhist mantra. You are also encouraged to remember the qualities of the Buddha at this time as these will inspire you to imitate Buddha's wisdom, skill and kindness in your daily life. You may also perform some analytic meditation where you think about the interpretation of the teachings of Buddha and apply these in your daily life. This can direct your energy towards an extremely positive direction first thing in the morning.

Quite often parents are faced with time constraints when it comes to meditation. They just do not seem to find the time to meditate since children are constantly calling for their attention. An effective way to begin your practice is by getting up earlier than your kids. That way you will be able to concentrate and meditate really early in the morning, setting the tone for the rest of the day. Another method of finding time to meditate is by involving children. Let them be near you – just explain that you need some quite time where you would not want to be disturbed. It is quite possible that your children also learn to meditate along with you. Otherwise, they can spend their time in constructive activities such as drawing, painting, reading etc.

It is good for children to watch their parents sit calm and still. It gives them the confidence to do the same. Imagine a stressed out household where mommy and daddy are running around all through the day – they get up finish their daily errands, rush to work, come back home, have dinner and crash in front of the TV. Kids become what they see. Would you want this kind of a lifestyle for your kids? Perhaps not!

If you want to cultivate great habits in children, you would need to practice them yourself. This means that you must care about yourself and be mindful of living a balanced and a healthy life.

You could even teach your children the correct manner to recite mantras or make offerings. I have seen four year old boys chant mantras when they get upset. They understand that these mantras can calm them down and bring immense satisfaction in their life. Some parents encourage children to make an offering of sweets or candies to the Buddha and in turn the children get a cracker or a piece of cake from Buddha. This instills in them a feeling of generosity and sharing.

PRACTICING DHARMA AT THE WORKPLACE

This seems impossible, correct? Is it possible to practice Dharma at workplace? Well, definitely yes! Let us see how.

When you set off for work after your morning meditation and breakfast, you remember the kind of positive motivation you had cultivated in your heart in the morning. You just need to remind yourself of your resolve to not harm anybody. Remind yourself several times during the day that you pledged not to harm anybody, be of service to your fellow human beings and that you will seek to perform all your actions for the ultimate awakening of yourselves and others.

There are various events that irritate us. You may want to use these as a trigger to remind you about the positive energy you instilled in yourself in the morning. So, instead of getting irritated at the traffic signal, think about how you had pledged that you would have a kind heart towards others. Before picking up that ringing telephone, remind yourself how you want to be of service to others. Use any trigger that works for you. I use the voice of my children as my trigger. Every time they call me, I remind myself of the kind heart that I have pledged to cultivate. And since this happens quite a number of times in a day, I am reminded of this a number of times in the day.

Throughout the day, try and develop mindfulness. Be aware of what you are thinking, saying, feeling, and doing, instead of living on "autopilot mode." When we live on autopilot mode, we react to various life situations naturally and instinctively. However, we do not get to experience what life is and what learnings these situations bring to us. This make us feel out of touch with our own self and we become strangers to our own self! Let me take an example of your drive to work. You drive to work every day, don't you? Now, if I ask you what is it that you think when you drive to work, you probably would not know the answer. A lot goes on in your mind and it does have an influence on your day, but being unmindful leads to unawareness of what is going inside your own mind and this is not a happy situation to be in!

CULTIVATING MINDFULNESS

Is there an antidote to living on an autopilot mode? Sure, there is! This is called mindfulness or awareness. Mindfulness means developing an awareness of what we are feeling, thinking, doing and saying each moment. It also implies being mindful of our kind heart and our ethical values, so that we can implement these in our everyday life. When you cultivate awareness, you develop conscious thinking and therefore you do not react to situations on an autopilot mode. You are no longer confused and exhausted without even understanding the reason of your confusion or exhaustion. The practice of mindfulness reminds you of your kind heart and empowers you to take all your actions based on that kind heart. Now, you may be irritated and angry, you may feel like shouting and screaming at somebody – but if you have a kind heart and are mindful of the situation around you, your kind heart will remind you to gather your breath and be aware of the present. You will notice your anger melt away in seconds.

BEING MINDFUL OF LIVING IN AN INTERDEPENDENT WORLD

Mindfulness can help us in every sphere of our life. You understand that you live in an interdependent world, don't you? Now, if you pollute the environment, you also cause harm to your children, family members, society and environment. And if you are mindful of being kind, you will automatically focus on curtailing the ways in which you pollute the environment. This may encourage you to think about options such as carpool as you go to work. You may start thinking about recycling paper, plastic containers, cans, newspapers, glass bottles and jars too. You do understand that throwing away these things in the garbage will impact your planet in a negative manner. Therefore, you will begin to re-use your plastic bags and paper bags. You will start switching off your air conditioners and heaters when you don't need them.

A number of monastic vows arose when people complained to Buddha about what monks and nuns were doing. Based on his observations, the Buddha defined certain percepts (you have read about these in the previous chapter). If he were alive today, he would definitely observe or receive complaints about the use of disposable plates, cups, cans etc. and not hesitate in defining a percept around it. He would try to curb this detrimental behavior by defining ways to recycle stuff and curtail consumption.

By bringing mindfulness in our actions towards the environment, we can make a positive difference to the environment.

BEING MINDFUL OF OUR ACTIONS

By developing mindfulness in actions, you develop understanding and compassion. Mindfulness encourages you to be aware of the reasons that are making you react in a particular manner and makes you ponder over alternative ways to react. Therefore, instead of getting angry, you think about the reason for your anger and if there can be another reaction. Awareness of the situation leads you to think from another person's point of view and deploy a strategy to be kind hearted at all times.

Now, how can you practice kind heartedness and mindfulness when a quarrel is about to begin? Well, that is the beauty of mindfulness meditation! It encourages you to practice beforehand and then, reminds you of being mindful when the actual situation arises. It just comes naturally to you! This is similar to a football team that trains and practices every day. This daily practices yields results on the big day! Similarly, the daily practice of mindfulness yields results when you need to actually practice it. It enables you to be mindful at all times.

OFFERING OUR FOOD

Did you know that offering the food that you consume is another way to elevate mindfulness and awareness? You must imagine your food to be blissful wisdom nectar. Think about it as something extremely delicious or something that enhances your wisdom. Next, imagine a small Buddha made of light placed at your heart. This Buddha radiates light that fills you up. Offer your food to this Buddha. And to do this, you don't even have to sit in a perfect meditative position! You can visualize and think about this small Buddha even when you are waiting for food.

A prayer may seem odd at a business meeting. But mindfulness teaches you methods to complete this offering. As your business associates and companions chat, you can complete the process of visualization and offering all by yourself, without anyone knowing it! As a family, you could recite a small prayer together before beginning to eat.

The next step is as you eat, eat mindfully! Develop awareness around the effort other people are putting into harvesting, transporting, and preparing your food. Think about your interdependence with other living beings and be thankful of the manner in which you have benefitted from this interdependence. The food you are eating is a result of this interdependence. Thinking about food in this manner will not only make you happy and grateful, it will make you mindful as well. And since you would be eating mindfully, you would never overeat! Wouldn't this lead to so much reduction in the expenses that you make in order to lose weight?

It is also important to eat in a dignified manner. Quite often, we see people queueing up in the cafeteria and grabbing the food even before they pay for it. This is being unmindful and non-dignified. When you know that you have to offer food to the Buddha, you become mindful and therefore, eat in a slow dignified manner. This is called as being aware of the food we are consuming along with the impact it will have on our body.

REVIEWING THE DAY

In this manner, you enrich your kind heart and maintain mindfulness as you move through your day. What do you do when you come home from work? Most individuals collapse in front of the TV or drop on their bed. It is a good idea to sit quietly for some time – all by yourself! During this time, you can reflect upon and come to terms with the happenings of the day. I encourage you to review your day and think about all the things that went well during the day along with the instances where you acted with a kind heart. Dedicate this merit to the positive force that guided you early morning and helped you in enlightenment of self and others.

As you review your day, you may discover that you were jealous, angry or greedy. You may not have realized this at the time of the actual occurrence. However, as you look back over your day, you do not feel nice or right about the manner in which you reacted. It could be something to do with your attitude, your actions or your speech! This may lead you to regret the happenings of the day. You can develop a purification practice to 'clean up' emotionally. This 'clean up' will lead you to a peaceful sleep. 'Clean up' can involve a number of actions – regret, reliance, remedial actions and a promise not to repeat the same behavior again. Try reflecting on your day every day and then practice 'clean up' as required. You will definitely notice a huge difference in your life!

As you prepare to sleep, visualize the Buddha sitting on your pillow. Put your head in Buddha's lap and prepare to rest. This is extremely comforting and relaxing. By simply doing this, you would feel that the Buddha has taken all your tensions and worries and is preparing you for the next day.

YOUR LIFE BECOMES MEANINGFUL

Practicing Dharma seems to be really difficult, doesn't it? In reality, it is not difficult at all. Remember, there will always be twenty four hours in a day. Directing your mind in a positive direction can enable you to transform your actions into the path of enlightenment. This way, Dharma will become a part of your life. You will get to experience Dharma in getting up in the morning, exercising, meditating, travelling to work, working, eating, sleeping –everything! You will be able to witness Dharma in all your relationships too! And this transformation of your attitude from an autopilot mode into mindfulness can make your life extremely meaningful!

Appreciating our advantageous circumstances and problems, leading our children by example and bringing Dharma in our daily lives can result in the creation of a meaningful society! And that is what Buddhists aim for!!!

LIVING IN THE PRESENT – MINDFULNESS AND MEDITATION

People turn to meditation for a number of reasons. Some people take to meditation in order to relieve stress. Others may begin to meditate in order to build in concentration. Buddhist meditation is far more serious than this. The practice of meditation encourages a Buddhist to develop awareness of how his mind is functioning. Meditation enables a Buddhist to tune in to every corner of the brain so that he can understand the ideas that are going through his mind. It helps him in controlling emotions and cultivating self-awareness.

You can choose to meditate in whatever manner you wish to. Zen meditation is the most popular form of meditation today. Here are some guidelines to Zen meditation or Zazen:

PLACE AND TIME

It is extremely important to find a time of the day when you would not be disturbed. An optimum place is important too. A number of people prefer to meditate just before or after their daily routine. Meditation in the morning can prepare you for the rest of the day. It also goes well with the Zen philosophy because the Zen mind believes that you should approach everything thinking that it is new. Mornings naturally signify new beginnings.

In the evening, Zazen can help you relax before you hit the bed. It is recommended that you practice meditation twice a day (morning and evening) so that you are better prepared for your day and also get some relaxation as you end the day. However, if you do not have that much time, you can choose any one time. Do not alternate between morning and evening as this may bring unrest. Initially you may need an alarm to remind you that your meditation time is over. This prevents you from the disturbance of watching the clock in the middle of a meditation session.

Define your place of meditation. It is recommended that you face a wall while you practice Zazen – it just diminishes distractions.

Another common question that people ask me is if they should meditate alone or in a community. Zen meditation retreats are termed as *sesshins*. These retreats help people connect amongst each other and practice meditation together. They also remind you that you are a part of the larger community or *sangha*, and this instills a sense of compassion towards your fellow human beings.

It is not necessary to meditate in lotus position (the lotus posture is the one where you sit with your legs interwined , right foot over your left thigh and left foot over your right thigh) only. You may want to sit on a chair or cross your legs. You may choose a position that is comfortable to you. It could be lotus, half lotus or the chair. I personally prefer the lotus posture because it reminds me that I am only doing Zazen at this time and everything else must wait. I only use the lotus posture while I meditate – never otherwise – it is my way of telling myself to be present!

Initially, if you are uncomfortable with your meditation posture, you may want to use a cushion or an exercise mat. Using a good meditation cushion can help a lot. A *zafu* (upper cushion) and a *zabuton* (lower cushion) are easily available in the market.

THE LOTUS POSTURE:

- Sit cross-legged on a cushioned surface
- Slowly, move your right leg and let it rest over your left knee. Your heel should be facing upwards
- Do the same with you left leg
- Place your hands such that they are one on top of other and your thumbs are touching your lap.
- Ensure that your back is straight and shoulders relaxed.
- Do not close your eyes tightly or keep them wide open. Aim for a middle posture with eyes too!

The Half Lotus posture:

- Cross your legs as you sit down on the floor.
- Next, bend your right leg until the sole rests on the inside of your left thigh.
- The calf of your right leg should be as close to the inside of your right thigh as you can.
- Bend your left leg until you can grab your left foot.
- Place it on the fold of your right leg and push your left knee as far down as possible.
- Place your hands above each other in the palm upright position. Some people prefer to let their hands rest on their knees with palms facing down. It is said that Buddha would keep one finger on the ground because he wanted to ask Earth to be a witness in his struggle for enlightenment.
- Ensure that your back is straight and shoulders relaxed.
- Do not close your eyes tightly or keep them wide open. Remember, you need to aim for a middle posture with eyes too!

Duration:

Zen believes that everyone is a beginner. It's just that some people are more beginner than the others. Therefore, they may experience a little more difficulty in maintaining posture and focus. Begin your initial meditation sessions with a daily practice of around five to ten minutes only. Initially, even five minutes may seem like a lot of time. I remember starting with three minutes only. Aim at increasing the duration of your meditation practice every week. Increase it up to twenty to thirty minutes or whatever works best for you. In some Zen centers, meditation is practiced for around forty five minutes. For me, twenty five minutes in the morning and ten minutes in the evening work best.

Remember, Zen is about finding your own self, it is about YOU! So, choose whatever suits best to you!

JUST SIT AND BREATHE

Meditation – seems like a heavy word, doesn't it? Well, let me first tell you that Zen meditation is not about trying to experience some kind of a trance, it does not get you into daydreaming and also does not ask you to control your thoughts. It leads you to experience without being judgmental. You are not supposed to analyze your thoughts and experiences. Because they are there – your senses are being triggered, just let them be like that. You will notice thoughts coming and going, do not follow them, just let them pass through!

Take the first few minutes to ground yourself. Analyze your posture. Are you comfortable and balanced? If not, switch to a comfortable posture. Can you hear the sounds that surround you? Can you also feel the ground beneath you and the air on your skin?

Now, move all your attention to your breath. Ensure that you are breathing deep through your abdomen and not shallow through your chest. Feel your breath. Do you feel it flowing through your nose, throat, belly? Great! Start counting! Count one – Inhalation through your nose, throat and belly; Count two – Exhalation through your belly, throat and nose; Count three – Inhalation once again – nose, throat, belly! Keep counting till ten. It is possible that you get engrossed in thoughts and therefore lose count! No problem, don't get mad at yourself! Just start again and count till the time you are able to count up to ten.

Do check your posture in between – just to be sure that you are sitting in the right manner. Try to sit as still as you can.

You can stop the process of counting your breaths and just focus on your breath –inhalation-exhalation-inhalation---and so on, once you gain some experience with meditation. This is the stage that you want to reach – the stage when you are doing nothing; you are 'just sitting'. You are not following your thoughts; you are only focusing on your breath!

And let me caution you, it does get boring at times. As you begin the process of meditation, your thoughts slow down, you start breathing slowly and deeply – you can get bored. Here comes what we call the self-discipline part of Zen. You will want to move, suddenly you may start feeling your body itch somewhere and you may get tempted to itch – wait! Do not move! This is how you are taming your mind to be ***self-disciplined.*** This is just your normal mind tantrum. You know how children throw tantrums at parents and teachers. And you also understand the rule that parents and teachers follow – they do not give in!

It is similar with your mind. Your mind is throwing tantrums at you – do not give in!

Do not stand up right after the alarm goes off. Take your time to slowly come back. Don't start thinking about your to do lists and action items right after your meditation session. Maintain your meditative state of mind for a few minutes post your meditation session too. Now, stand up and begin your next task. Just remember, that you need to start any task with the same mindfulness and awareness as you started Zazen.

Because mindfulness in all your actions will lead you to experience Zen!

Bringing mindfulness in all your deeds and ensuring that you carry Zazen in all your actions enables you to remain in a state of perpetual meditation. This is the state of total awareness and immersion in the present moment. This may seem impossible at the moment, especially if you have just started and are still struggling with your ten minute Zazen practice. However, this is not impossible. Try and stick to the practice and in some time, you will be glad you did!

HAVING FAITH

The practice of Zen and Buddhism as a whole requires huge faith.

You want to be mindful, don't you? So, you need to have faith that life is something you should pay attention to.

You want to practice meditation, don't you? Therefore, you need to have faith that it is worth the effort!

You want to achieve inner peace, don't you? Therefore, you need to have faith that you are complete and there is peace inside you. You have to believe that you have achieved perfection and this has created inner peace inside you.

It is alright if you do not believe some of these things at the moment. Just take them on faith. This is journey that focuses on discovering yourself. Believe in yourself; believe that you are complete and that mindfulness and meditation are only making you discover your true self!

Pure faith can work wonders for you in this journey of self-discovery.

MEDITATING ON KOANS

Koans are no longer alien to Westerners. In fact, it seems to be the most familiar technique to practice Zen meditation. How would you describe koans? Well, koans cannot be described! Sounds silly and illogical, correct? That's what koans are!

They seem to be illogical and paradoxical; they are the non sensical questions, stories or anecdotes that should be pondered upon until they are understood at a level beyond reasoning. Koans can tame the wandering mind and enable you reach a state of enlightenment.

A number of Zen practitioners do not use koans, but some find them extremely helpful. They serve as tools that enable you to reach your full potential. Some people like to call them gateways to self. Koans can become your mantra to live by, if you just use them as a reminder that life is not about rules or logic. Sometimes, there is logic in things that do not make sense and are completely illogical.

You may wish to practice meditating on koans all by yourself or under the guidance of a Zen teacher. Many Westerners try and interpret the meaning of koans on their own and start practicing without discussing or presenting their answers to anybody. Some students, however, try and begin practicing koans under the guidance of a teacher who assigns a particular koan to his/ her student. This is termed as *Dokusan* – a private meeting between a student and a teacher where the student gets to understand the koan, ask questions and present answers.

Meditation on a koan sometimes present its unique challenges – especially when you do not use the teacher methodology to interpret the koan. If you ever feel that you are stuck during the process of contemplating a koan, let it just go on in your mind. Indulge in something that is more active. Did you know that at times physical activities can lead to enlightened answers to all your dilemmas – career choices, relationships or even koans?

Koans also encourage you to be in the moment – they may sound silly and trying to understand them intellectually is not actually understanding them Each person may interpret koans in their own different ways. A teacher can let you know if you have really understood the koan. But, don't worry, if you don't want to go down the teacher route, you can try and perceive an answer to your koan at an intuitive level.

KARMA AND REINCARNATION

Karma is an important concept of Buddhism and is strongly connected to reincarnation. Buddhism believes that each individual is reincarnated again and again until this individual attains Nirvana. The literal meaning of the word 'karma' is action. This implies that every action that we perform has an impact on our future. You may call Karma as an architect for your future or a descriptor of your past. It is your actions, thoughts and intents – all combined together.

A Buddhist aims at getting out of the vicious cycle of Karma in order to attain enlightenment. It is believed that Karma can impact the place where you will be reincarnated. It is said that good karma can lead you to be reincarnated in a good place and bad karma can lead you to be reincarnated in a bad place.

Karma is influenced by your day to day actions. Actions based on the principles of truth, selflessness, generosity, kindness, wisdom and mindfulness will lead to good karma. Destructive actions based on materialism, fallacies and greed will lead to bad karma.

The concept of Karma should be understood as one of the natural laws of nature. The primary objective of Buddhism lies in helping you gain control over your actions, which in turn impact your Karma.

Therefore, Buddhists lay great emphasis on mindfulness and encourage you to 'be present', 'aware' or 'mindful' of things around you.

Practice and self-discipline can lead your actions towards good karma and hence reincarnation!

Thank You

Before you go, I want to warmly say "thank you" from the bottom of my heart! I realize that there are many e-books on the market and you decided to purchase this one so I am forever grateful for that.

Thanks a million for reading this book all the way to very end!

If you enjoyed this book then I need your help!

Please take a moment to leave a review for this book after you turn the page.

This valuable feedback will allow me to write e-books that help you in your journey through life. And if you love it, please let me know.

Made in the USA
Middletown, DE
19 June 2017